The Divorced Men's Survival Guide

By Greg Fisher

TABLE OF CONTENTS

DEDICATION

This book is dedicated to my inner circle of friends to whom I owe everything. If not for their encouragement, patience and love…I'm not sure where I would be right now.

Thank you so much Bill, Kerry, Skippy, Scotty, Kelly, Lois, Dre and Susan. You will always have a special place in my heart and my gratitude.

INTRODUCTION

I was happily married for 15 years...unfortunately, my marriage lasted 19 years. When my wife asked me (told me) that we were getting divorced, I was emotionally stunned. To say that I was domestically challenged would be an understatement.

Had it not been for my good friend, Gary Schumer taking me in, I'm not sure how this story would have turned out. For that, I will be forever in his debt. Now back to my story: I was separated from my children and the only woman I'd ever loved. Money was tight (as it always is at this time). Most people don't realize that when a marriage ends, for a while there are two households to support. I was depressed. In short, I was lost.

After searching the Internet time and time again, I found that there wasn't much out there to help divorced men cope with a changing life; I decided to write about my own experiences and tell you how I learned to deal with things.

We all know that men are supposed to be the tough guys and be able to care for themselves…I say "bullshit" to that thought. We have feelings too. We might not ask for directions but I'm going to offer help if you want it.

I'm told that 41% of marriages end in divorce and since a little more than 2 million people get married each year, basic math tells us that there's about 400,000 newly divorced guys every year in the United States. Let that sink in…that's almost enough guys to fill up Yankee Stadium for 10 games! That's a lot of hot dogs in one stadium.

This book is written from my own experiences, period. I make no claims that I have a PhD in anything. I will tell you what has worked for me and let you learn from my mistakes and triumphs. I'm not guaranteeing that what I did will work for you, but heck, it should. Just plan on tweaking it to fit your style.

Now, I know that everyone wants to skip ahead to the chapter "How to get laid." Hey, it was fun to write (not to mention doing all of the research) and it's a great read. Personally, I think the most important chapter is called "Adjustment." I urge you to read that chapter several times because there's a lot more to divorce than getting your pole waxed.

With that being said, I will honestly tell you that I will be really disappointed if what you learn in this book doesn't help you sow some wild oats...LOL. I know that many of these ideas work not only for me but for many of my friends as well. Follow what I say with a grain of salt. If you don't feel comfortable, chances are it might not be right for you. Listen to your gut.

Remember 3 Things:

1. It will be okay. Life isn't over because of your divorce.
2. Readjust your focus and choose to be happy.
3. You're not alone in this even if sometimes you feel you are.

Good luck and I'm looking forward to hearing your story. Please share it with me at: divorced-men.com.

Sincerely,

Greg Fisher

ADJUSTMENT

So you're recently divorced. I know how tough that can be. There are a lot of guys that have been in the same situation so take comfort in the fact that you're not alone.

I know that last statement doesn't mean much to make you feel better. I had a counselor once tell me that if I was lying in a hospital bed with a sprained ankle and the guy in the next bed had a broken ankle, the fact that the guy next to me was hurt more severely didn't make my pain feel any less. It took me a year to figure out what that crazy bastard meant; turns out he was right.

I will never discount your pain and neither should you. Allow yourself some time to grieve the loss of your marriage. Hell, it's like someone died! Take your time to get over it. But…don't take too much time. You only have so many days on the calendar and so many ticks on the clock. I urge you not to waste them but LIVE them.

My dad used to say to me "Son, laugh and the world will laugh with you. Cry and you'll cry alone." It's a very true statement. Ask yourself this: would you rather hang out with a buddy that was fun or a buddy that was depressed all of the time? It's honestly that simple….don't be the depressed buddy or you will be alone. My suggestion is to take no more than a maximum of six weeks to mourn. If you're done sooner, great. If it takes you a little longer, that's also fine. If you're going on 4 months or more, then you may need to seek some professional help because no one deserves to live that way.

Here's some practical advice: if you're just separated, don't sign a lease on a place to live. Stay with friends or family until you know if you can work things out with your wife. Don't pay for another place if there's a chance that you can get your relationship back. I certainly urge you to try. One option is to look for a roommate. Place a post on Facebook or put an ad on Craigslist. The first year is the hardest. If you can share expenses and have someone around to keep you from being lonely…then that's even better.

As I mentioned in the Introduction, I moved in with my buddy Gary for a couple of weeks. After two weeks, I asked for another two weeks. After those two weeks, he said it would be great if I just stayed. He was separated and on his own like me. It was good for both of us to have someone around as an 'in house' support specialist. Eventually, our buddy Scott moved in with us and Gary's house became known as the "Frat House." In fact, we still call it that even though we don't live there anymore.

I would tell you stories about those days, but I'd have to change the names to protect the innocent. Only problem is that I don't think there were any "innocent" people partying at the Frat House…LOL. There always seemed to be something going on there when I didn't have my daughter over for the night.

Remember: If you live with someone else make sure that their characteristics are similar to yours. Some things to ask yourself: Do they have kids like me? Do they have similar schedules (I work early and he's a night owl)? Will they keep up their end, financially? Are they a pig when I am a neat freak? Are they a dick? Do I really like hanging around with this person? Don't put yourself in a bad situation. If a potential roommate isn't the right fit for you, don't do it just to do it. Fortunately, it worked for me; actually it worked out great for all of us because we enjoyed life, saved money, shared the chores around the house and we were not lonely.

Some women didn't think it was cool to date me because of my living arrangements but I didn't really care. If they were that uptight over that then they weren't right for me anyway. Don't get caught up on what some women think is acceptable. They are always going to try to change you anyway so enjoy your freedom while you have it.

<u>Here are 3 things I learned after my divorce:</u>

1. I get myself into the right frame of mind. When I'm going on a sales call, business meeting or date, I always do this: I pull my car into a parking lot, lean back in my seat and close my eyes. I tell myself over and over again that I'm a quality person who is smart, fun to be around and that people like me for a reason. Then I imagine that 'spirit' coming out of me like a pheromone until it's tangible and something that people actually react to. Something that I can use to influence them. I honestly believe that I emit a pheromone

that people react to and as proof…I close about 2/3 of all of my sales calls on the first meeting and over 90% on the second meeting.

2. The second thing I do is much harder to do than the first. I actually saw this in a Jennifer Aniston movie which title I never bothered to learn. But the lead guy in the movie starts each day by smiling like an idiot for 5 minutes straight. It's tough to do, trust me. But when you can get yourself to that point, you will start to smile easier and be more approachable to others. People will be drawn to you and you'll be in a better mood. I know, I know, it sounds hokey. But it works for me. Give it a shot for a few weeks. It will take you that long to build up the muscles in your face to smile for that long. I promise that you will be amazed at the results.

3. The last thing that I do every day is what I call the moment of truth. I'm not sure if you're aware of this or not but you can't lie to yourself successfully. You can always call the bullshit factor on yourself. Here's how it works: Each morning look in the bathroom mirror and stare into your own eyes. Hold the gaze until you answer one simple question, "What will make me happy today?" Keep holding that stare. It's very important to lock your eyes onto yourself until you answer. It's not easy. It takes concentration and practice but it will give you something that a lot of divorced guys don't have right away.....direction. You'll know which way to go. FYI don't do this at the same time you're doing the smiling thing in step 2.

It's important to take yourself out of your comfort zone. Get off of the couch. If you're broke and can't afford to do anything take a walk. Just get off your ass and away from the TV and/or computer. You need this time away. Don't do the easy thing. Do the right thing for yourself.

Try playing a musical instrument. I play guitar (not well). Spend some time each day practicing that. It will pay huge dividends for you later. If you need some incentive, women LOVE a man that can play an instrument (and not your own instrument either perve).

If you take lessons, ask for an instructor that will simply teach you how to play songs. Don't learn the stupid scales and other crap, at first. Just learn to play the songs that you like. For example, I can play about ten songs on my guitar pretty well. That's it. I don't know how to read music. Couldn't play any notes if you bet me to. But I can play a song and sing the words to Johnny Cash, the Beatles, American Pie and a few others pretty well. In fact, I've been laid from being able to do that about 10 times! So don't waste your time in the beginning learning all of the stuff you don't need. If it comes easily to you then great, but work on what pays off.

Later in the book, I'm going to teach you how to prepare simple meals. I've learned to love cooking since my divorce. I'm not going to start you out with difficult things to make but easy dishes that are healthy and taste great. I've also learned that women

LOVE men that can cook. So be ready to put on that masculine apron, fellas!

One thing I don't want you doing is eating out every night, going to bars, drinking too much, eating crap frozen pizzas and making yourself unhealthy. If you're not taking a multiple vitamin every day then start NOW! Give it a month or so to hit your system and you'll be shocked at how much better you feel. I'll go over this a little later in the "Getting Ready and Ratings" chapter.

I noticed that I lost a lot of friends in my divorce. I often joke with friends that I still have from when I was married and tell them that I was awarded custody of them in the divorce. It's difficult for me and my ex to keep the same friends. We try to keep our lives private from each other. Outside of our children. we have very little contact. With that said, you may need to make some new friends.

Try Meetup.com. What this site does is put you in touch with people that share your interests. I've seen them do everything from kickball, volleyball and softball teams to music, dancing and movie groups. Someone is in charge of the group and they plan events and then list them on a page that you're a member of (there's no cost for this service in my area). You simply pick what events that you want to do.

I've had the opportunity to date people from this group but I never have. I didn't want to mess up people that I could do social things with. I take dates to certain events and simply show up for others looking to have a good time. It beats sitting at home on the couch. Also, don't jump into another relationship. I had a transition person. Many people do. It's common for both sexes to try it out with another person and then realize that they don't want to be with them and pull out before marriage. Don't rush it. Take your time and date. There are more single women than men.

Finally, the last thing I've learned to do (or it may be the first thing you do) since getting divorced is to quiet your mind and pray. Yes, I'm spiritual. I'm not going to preach to you. Don't believe me? Piss, cocksucker, pussy, tits, homo, fucker, shit head.....see? I'm spiritual but not religious. If you feel comfortable going to your church then by all means, don't stop. I actually encourage it because it gives you a larger sense of purpose. I go to church. But I also know that God lives everywhere, not just in a building with a cross on top of it.

Here are 8 things learned in this chapter:

1. Make sure the relationship is over.
2. Grieve the loss of the relationship.
3. Look into getting a compatible roommate.
4. Do the 3 exercises that I gave you daily.
5. Take yourself out of your comfort zone.
6. Learn to play an instrument or cook.
7. Pray to a higher power.
8. Chances are that you will have to add people to your circle of friends.

Please remember this line because I will end each chapter with it…you're not alone in this even if sometimes you think you are.

SETTING UP HOUSE

This is by far the hardest chapter for me to write. It's not easy setting up a household alone, guys. So I'm going to take you through it room by room – bedroom, laundry (where all cleaning junk is), bathroom and finally, the kitchen (which is the most involved). Lastly, in this chapter I'm going to give you some simple decorating advice. Trust me, I'm not a designer but I have dated several women who are.

Please note that I did all of my pricing at one national department store (Target) and that I live in the Midwest where prices are lower. I took everything I purchased and converted it into today's dollars by comparing new online prices. I can't stress enough that you should look through thrift stores, garage sales or you may come across extra stuff from friends and relatives.

Take your mom, sister, aunt or any other female you know with you shopping. Why? Because they LIVE for this shit! Don't let them decorate your space (unless you absolutely have no sense of style) and if you don't like their suggestions, don't use them. Case in point, my mom makes a great meatloaf and is awesome in the kitchen but I would feel extremely uncomfortable having a million angel figurines and strawberry patterned wallpaper staring me each morning while I drank my coffee. So go with YOUR taste on flatware and place ware. For example: I have simple tastes so all of my plates and bowls are plain white.

But I'm moving ahead too far. I told you I'd start with the bedroom, so here we go…first, I'm going to assume that you have a bed, night stand, dresser/chest, sheets and pillows from the divorce. If you didn't, well, you need those things. I went through my first separation sleeping on an air mattress and it totally screwed up my back, I don't advise this.

For a bedroom, you will basically need an alarm clock, curtains (get the inexpensive ones in two sets of white or whatever other color you like), hangers (you can fit a lot of clothes in the closet and they stay better looking longer), a comforter or blanket for your bed. Now because I had such a small room, I put my bed on lifts (I bought a set for $20 at Bed Bath and Beyond) and then I could put a lot of extra crap underneath my bed. I picked up something called a bed skirt which covers the area from the box springs to the floor so people can't see all that extra crap under the bed. Now get yourself some big ass Tupperware bins and you can store extra clothes, shoes, mementos, receipts and you name it, under your bed and out of the way.

Trust me, women like organized spaces. If you have clothes and crap all over your room, plan on playing a lot of away games because the girls won't come (or cum) in clutter. Keep your clothes clean and use hangers as much as possible. When you get home, immediately hang up your shirts and pants so you don't have to iron or dry clean every time you wear them. Buy Fabreeze and give them a quick squirt before you put them back in your closet.

Ok…and speaking of clothes, on to the laundry room. I keep all cleaning stuff there and put additional shelving in for my extra canned goods, food items in glass jars, Tupperware, paper plates and cups. I'll be quite honest with you…I don't clean my own house. I have a cleaning lady that comes by every 2 weeks to do it. I also don't launder my dress shirts or nice slacks at home. I get them dry cleaned and pressed. I actually do own an iron but that's just for pressing t-shirts. All I wash at home is the basic stuff like blue jeans, t-shirts, socks, underwear, towels and sheets.

I really try to keep my life simple. I HATE cleaning the house. So even though money is tight, it's something that I chose to splurge on. I pay $100 a month to have my place cleaned twice a month. All of the beds are changed and the sheets are laundered for that price too. Again, TO ME it is money well spent.

A couple of things to remember when/if you do your own laundry: Don't do towels with any other items that you want to keep looking nice. I keep the water temperature always on cold for everything. There's no need to switch it to hot for whites. I put my sheets in separately as well. I throw everything else in together. That's right…white shirt with red shirt, jeans with underwear. It honestly doesn't matter. Most detergents today are color sensitive and the reds (usually) don't turn your white shirt pink, if you wash it together. So don't worry about it.

You can stock your laundry room with bleach (great for cleaning sinks and pouring down stinky drains), detergent, glass cleaner, Lysol, oven cleaner, wood floor cleaner (if you have wood floors), carpet stain remover and any other cleaning products that either you or anyone cleaning, prefers. I also keep my mops, brooms, Swiffer bowl scrubbers and other assorted crap there.

I'm also presuming that you have a washer and a dryer. If you don't, they will set you back about $1500 for a good set. Remember to clean the lint trap on your dryer every other load or it can be a fire hazard. Don't dry things that are 'Dri-fit.' Just put them on a hanger and let them air dry. You're also going to need a couple of clothes hampers for dirty clothes. I just use large laundry baskets.

Well, that's about all I can think of for the laundry room, so let's move on to the second most important room in the house, the bathroom. Women TOTALLY examine your bathroom. I mean, let's face it...WE look at their bathrooms, too. Well, I do anyway. I don't like women that wear a lot of makeup; I think that they're high maintenance. So when invited to a woman's house, I will check out their bathrooms to see what all they have to do each night before they go to bed. My point? Well, if we're doing it then they are too.

There are a few simple things to make your bathroom look nicer and be a little more organized. Try getting some small baskets to put things in like shaving cream, extra razors, aftershave lotion, etc. When women come over, put that basket in a closet or under the sink to clear off clutter. Wipe the piss off of the toilet seat with toilet paper and water. Make sure the sink is wiped out and put your towels away. An easy thing to do that makes them think you're not a pig is to simply put an air freshener in the bathroom. Not kidding…they will notice and may even comment on that. One last trick I do in the bathroom is brush my teeth in the shower. It clears away that junk off of my counter and keeps the crap out of my sink.

Now we come to the meat of this chapter…the big one…the room that will cost you not only money but can decide a big part of your future…the kitchen. The kitchen is where most people hang out in when you have a party. It's where you put fuel into the greatest machine you'll ever own …your body. It's where your house becomes a home. It can also get you laid.

And, since this chapter is called “Setting Up House”, let’s get to setting up the kitchen. We’ll talk some simple recipes that will make you look like a hero later. But first you have to have the tools to build a house. Here are the tools that you’ll need. Let me repeat this one more time…I priced everything new from Target. Look around for deals at thrift stores or garage sales. Not everything has to be brand new.

That being said to set up a kitchen you’re going to spend about $800. I know that it might sound expensive but consider this. If you go out for a meal for one, it’s going to cost you (depending on where you eat) not less than $10. The average cost of a homemade meal is around $2 per serving. So if you make just 15 meals at home per week (think breakfast, lunch and dinner Monday-Friday) you will pay off your kitchen in about 6 ½ weeks! PLUS you will eat better meals that are healthier (less fat and sodium) and it will help you get laid too. If you have kids, there's nothing better than making a meal with them to not only teach them how to cook but to bond with them.

Ok…if I haven't sold you enough on the kitchen's importance by now then just move on to the next chapter. However, if you realize how important it is to have a kitchen to make a house a home then you're going to need these tools:

Small Appliances

Microwave	$100
Blender	$35
Toaster	$25

Crock pot	$20
Coffee maker	$20

Now the place that you move into may have a microwave and instead of a toaster, you may want to get a toaster oven (approximately $15 more…it's more versatile but it takes up counter space). A crock pot will become your best friend and I don't know about you, but I don't want to think about a day without coffee.

These items you can often find at garage sales and thrift shops so rather than spending $200 for brand new items you can probably buy them all for $100 or less, used.

Now let's move onto more basic tools for your kitchen. Again, same pricing points, I shopped at Target to get my prices but a lot of this shit you CAN find at second hand stores, garage sales or from friends/relatives. Also, the quality may be higher than a new product too!

Additional Kitchen Gadgets:

Pot holders (4)	$8	Dish towels	$10
Canister Set	$20	Flatware organizer	$20
Baking Pans (2)	$30	Drawer organizers	$20
Baking sheets (2)	$15	Pizza Pan	$10
Knife set	$100	Colander	$10
Mixing bowls (3)	$20	Large handled bowls	$20
Cookware set	$80	Measuring cups	$6
Scissors	$2	Filtered pitcher	$25
Flatware set	$40	Plate & bowl set (8)	$60

Cups & glasses	$30	Wine glasses (4)	$20
Can opener	$6	Bottle opener	$2
Spatula (2)	$15	Wisk	$5
Serving spoons (4)	$12	1 gallon pitchers (2)	$28
Cutting board	$15	Pizza cutter	$3
Salad tongs	$8	Meat fork & tongs	$10

Okay, so here are a couple of other hints:

1. Don't buy cheap spatulas.
2. Look for combo sets to cut costs.
3. Get a big vase to put your cooking utensils (stuff) in.
4. You will use throw away Tupperware a lot.

Base Spices and Sauces

Make sure that you have these spices (look for a big spice rack for cost savings but realize that it takes up counter space and you won't use most of them).

Steak sauce

Shrimp cocktail sauce

Horseradish

Ketchup

Mustard (also get brown spicy)

Salt

Pepper

Sugar

Artificial sweeteners (Sweet and Low packets)

Vanilla

Olive oil (don't worry about the virgin)

Garlic salt

Mrs. Dash

Greek seasoning

Salsa (get chunky and smooth)

Keep a stock of these at all times because you will use them often. These items will for a long time and only a few of them will need to be kept in the fridge after you open them.

Misc

Last thing for your kitchen …these items, like the spices will have to be replaced as you use them but by always having them on hand will make your life much easier.

Plastic wrap

Disposable Tupperware

Zip lock bags

Toothpicks

Aluminum foil

Now you are ready….these basics will put you in the position to start…so START!!! If you think your first meals will be great…think again. It takes practice to get good at anything. If you screw up a meal, so what? Throw it away and start again. The journey in this case IS half of the fun. When you get good at cooking a meal and can do it easily, then invite a lady over to serve her wine while you don the apron…play your cards right and by the end of the evening she'll be taking off of you more than the apron and putting more than your cooking in her mouth.

I'd love to hear your success stories, your recipes and tips. Send them to me at: divorced-men.com. If you think I know it all, think again! As I will keep telling you, I know what has worked for me. That's what I'm sharing with you.

Remember that you're not alone in this even if sometimes you think you are.

Simple Meals and Recipes

Most women are foodies. They not only like to go out to eat but they like to enjoy food prepared for them by someone else. If you're lucky, you'll find a woman that likes to cook too. Side note: Women and men differ in foods very, very, very much! I will say it in a different way in case you missed it. WOMEN AND MEN DIFFER IN THEIR FOOD CHOICES A LOT!!!

No biggie though…we just have to be adaptable. For instance, when serving a meal that you've made, give her a child's serving of food. Make sure that you're serving a well-rounded meal (this is good advice for you to do daily as well). Your health starts in the kitchen. How you shop, what meals you prepare, your diet and what fuels you put into your body will make you not only look better but actually make you feel better too. Does it take extra effort? Yes. Is it worth it? You bet your ass it is!!!

With what I've already written, I hope I've convinced you that diet is an important part of your life...AND your sex life too! I will talk to you later about exercise. Impress the ladies with your staying power in the bedroom. Well, what ends in the bedroom starts in the kitchen. I honestly don't know how many times I've been laid because I'm a good cook. But it's been a lot.

Before we begin to cook we have to learn how to shop for food. It's called meal planning and after you learn how to do it, it's quite simple. Most guys get screwed up at the grocery store.

Here's a quick reference for you to remember:

- Easy-to-make kits = either expensive or fattening (like frozen pizza, lasagnas or pot pies). They just have so many preservatives and are made with fat so that they taste decent.
- Canned = high in sodium (salt), preservatives and fat.

Now, of course I've had these. I will even recommend using canned products later. If you can, always go fresh. Canned, boxed and frozen is good for a quick meal but if you want to be lean and healthy and get laid, please do it my (now, "our") way…your call.

Meal planning means that you buy enough groceries for a set number of meals at home. Some of the ingredients for these meals overlap and you'll use them for more than one meal…so when you're buying things like olive oil, milk, salt, butter or eggs, be sure to think about what you want to make during the week. Stay away from the wholesale food clubs to buy bulk food. It's not fresh. It doesn't really taste good. It's not good for you. It's just easy.

This chapter has taken me a ton of work to put together. I try to keep things simple. K I S S = keep it simple shithead…learn it, know it, live it……Simple means simple…feel free to tweak these recipes to your taste. They don't take long to prepare. I keep the ingredients to a bare minimum. They all keep well so you can use your Tupperware for leftovers and to save some money.

Apron on? Here we go!!!

Southern Sweet Tea

This may sound goofy but making this is an art and I promise you, that women love this.

Take one of your new gallon pitchers and fill it halfway up with water and pour that into a pot with a heaping cup of sugar (adjust it to your taste with more or less) and 2 drops of vanilla (not more or it will be bitter). Bring it to a boil, turn off the heat and add 2 large or 5 small teabags to the pot. Let it steep in the pot for 10 minutes. Pour the water back into your pitcher (put the pitcher in the sink in case you spill any) and then fill the rest of the pitcher with cold water. Put the pitcher in the fridge and when it cools, it's ready to serve. DONE!

- To make hot tea on-the-go for a lady, pour the tea into a coffee cup and nuke it for about 2 minutes.
- For an Arnold Palmer (my favorite drink) make a pitcher of lemonade from a concentrate and mix it 50/50. It not only tastes great but it's an impressive drink and makes you look like an apron wearing stud!

Asparagus

It might make your pee smell stinky but it's an awesome aphrodisiac (sex fuel) for both of you. It's also a great side dish that will make you look like a chef.

Heat your oven to 500 degrees, fill you baking pan with asparagus, and generously coat them with olive oil, pepper and a little garlic salt. Bake for 10 minutes. DONE!

- This is a great side dish with fish, beef or pork. Not chicken or turkey because it will overwhelm their flavor.
- Fresh asparagus is best, not canned or frozen.

Hawaiian Chicken

I use chicken tenders but you can also use boneless, skinless breasts. Spray your baking pan with cooking spray (use a lot). Spread the thawed chicken out in the pan and pour an entire of 12 oz bottle of Hawaiian dressing (this is found by the salad dressing in your grocery store or ask for it) on top of the chicken. Bake for 20 minutes at 350 degrees. DONE!

- Great alternative to BBQ sauce.
- This dish can also be grilled.
- If you overcook this, it will dry out the chicken.

Panko Parmesan Tilapia

From any major grocery store, look for Panko chips (Japanese bread crumbs) and parmesan garlic sauce. Pour your Panko chips into a bowl. Take your tilapia filets and rub the parmesan garlic sauce into them. Put your filets into the bowl with the Panko chips and turn them over to coat them on both sides. Again, using your baking pan, spray it with a lot of cooking spray. Place the filets in the baking pan. Bake at 410 degrees for 12-15 minutes. DONE!

- Try this meal with an ice cold bottle of Riesling wine and ice water.
- Goes great with Uncle Ben's cheddar broccoli rice.

Bacon Wrapped Filets

Here's what you're going to use: 2 boneless filets of steak, 2-4 pieces of bacon, liquid smoke, Kitchen Bouquet and toothpicks. All the ingredients you're gonna need for a party in your mouth.

Rinse the filets with water (always wash packing preservatives off of all meat). Rinse your bacon. Put both on a plate and pour liquid smoke and Kitchen Bouquet over the filets. Take the bacon and go around the filet like a ribbon on a wrapped gift. Secure the bacon to filet with a toothpick. Bake on your cooking pan at 350 degrees for 20 minutes. DONE!

- Great with steamed broccoli, a loaded baked potato and a California Table Red wine with ice tea or water.
- This is an uber masculine meal. Even though it tastes great, don't expect a lot of credit because men are supposed to "know" steak.
- I buy bacon on sale and freeze it.

Special Shrimp Cocktail Sauce

Show her that you put the extra effort in everything you do. She will notice that your sauce is homemade and not just from a bottle. It will not only make her feel special, but will make her mouth water (hopefully, for some of YOUR special sauce).

Most shrimp cocktail sauces come in a 12 oz. bottle. Pour half of the bottle- of an inexpensive cocktail sauce into a bowl. Put 2 tablespoons of horseradish and mix thoroughly. DONE!

- Not only does this taste amazing but it will clear your sinuses.
- This will work for about a dozen shrimp. So if you need more…make more.

Cajun Butter Bombs

The name of this dish is very misleading…it just sounds cool to me. For 2 people, take 2 pieces of tilapia/cod/ catfish/swai or any type of white fish (so don't use salmon).

Get some Cajun breading and pour into a mixing bowl. Rinse off the filets (because you want them to be wet to hold the breading) and put it in a bowl with the breading. Roll them around in the bowl until covered. Place them in your baking pan that's (you guessed it) coated with a lot of cooking spray. Sprinkle a little paprika on top and bake at 400 degrees for 15 minutes. After taking it out of the over, hit it with a ton of spray butter. DONE!

- Serve this with a cold Chardonnay and ice water.
- I like to serve this with salad and brown rice.

Steamed Milk Coffee

Everyone goes to Starbucks and pays $4 for a cup of coffee. Café Misto is basically steamed milk with coffee. Wanna make it at home for about 20 cents?

In your coffee cup, fill it with about 1/3-1/2 of milk (any kind of milk…skim, 2%, whole…whatever). Nuke it for about 30 seconds and then put coffee on top of it. DONE!

- Try flavored creamer to change it up.
- Try using a high quality flavored coffee. I like Highland Grog but use whatever YOU like.
- This will not work well with soy milk.

Steamed Broccoli

2 pounds of broccoli only costs $3 so buy the fresh stuff. Frozen is okay but hear me now and understand me later…when she sees you cutting up fresh broccoli for her, prepare to get lucky after dinner.

First, wash your broccoli. Then pull out YOUR new cutting board. Take one of your manly sharp knives and cut off the broccoli heads. Throw away the stems. Put the broccoli heads into your large glass mixing bowl and fill it halfway with water. Nuke it on high for 5 minutes. When it's done cooking, drain the water and put a lot of butter on top of the broccoli. It will melt and soak it. DONE!

- Broccoli makes a great side dish for fish, chicken, beef and pork.
- It's good for you and I've been told it makes your cum actually taste good. I have NO knowledge of that firsthand because I'm NOT a pole smoker but what the hell…eat it for her!

Loaded Baked Potato

Whenever my daughter has friends over, this is the meal they want me to make them. I'm always shocked that 12 year old girls can eat 2-3 large loaded baked potatoes while watching horror movies and messing up my living room. To makes this, you're gonna need: 2 large baked potatoes, shredded cheddar cheese, butter, sour cream and bacon bits.

First, wash the potatoes and stab them with a knife 3-4 times each. You don't have to go in further than ¼ inch. Microwave the potatoes on high for 7 minutes. Now comes the tricky part…slice the potatoes on the top from one end to the other, about ½ ways through the potato. Squeeze the potato until it pops and then use a fork to pull the meal (inside of the potato) away from the skin. Put a full tablespoon of butter and sour cream on each potato. Then fill the top of the potato with cheese and cover them with bacon bits. Nuke them again for another 90 seconds. DONE!

- This is a great side dish for steak.
- It also is a good meal by itself. Serve with a cold beer, if you're eating it as a meal.
- If you wanna get really fancy, fry some bacon to a crisp and crumble it on top of the potato (I rarely fry bacon inside because it makes the house smell like bacon and even though guys like the smell of bacon, sadly enough, it doesn't equal SEXY to women).
- You can add leftover broccoli to this to make it a more complete meal.

Chocolate Crème Pie

This is a quick and easy desert that you can brag about. Take it to a party and tell everyone that you made it from scratch…well…kind of. You only need a few ingredients…a pie shell (that's already in a foil container), a box of chocolate Jell-O, a little butter and generic cool whip.

Make a box of Jell-O chocolate pudding. The directions are on the box…read it. It only takes about a half a cup of milk that you boil. Trust me; if you can't make Jell-O, then you shouldn't be in a kitchen. While the Jell-O is cooking, take 5 pats of butter and put on the pie shell. Bake it in the oven at 300 degrees for about 5 minutes. After the Jell-O is done, scoop it into the pie shell and use the BACK of a spoon to spread it evenly in the pie shell. Press it down so there are no air pockets. Put a ton of whip cream on top of the pudding…take your time to make it to look pretty. DONE!

- Doesn't matter what kind of milk that you use.
- Get the generic whip cream. It will save you a buck and any extra may come in handy in the bedroom!
- Put the pie in the fridge for at least 2-3 hours before serving so the pudding cools.

Irish Coffee

This is a kick ass drink if you're going to an outdoor soccer game or a fall picnic. Something that will warm you up, make you smile, tastes good and chicks…LOVE it!

We're going to use the same formula that we used with our steamed coffee recipe. You're going to use an Irish cream whiskey. Some popular ones are Bailey's and Bushmill's but there are a ton of generic ones out there that are less expensive and taste just as good. Fill a coffee cup about 1/3 of the way with Bailey's, nuke for 30 seconds and top with coffee. If you have whipped cream, use it. DONE!

- If you're using a thermos, DO NOT add whip cream…it will screw up your thermos.
- Perfect for wake and bake events.
- Try adding a shot of vodka for every 3 cups for more kick! If you use too much vodka, it will ruin the taste.

Crock Pot Beef Stew

I make a lot of meals with my crock pot (it's a slow cooker NOT a pressure cooker). It's easy and time saving. You can put your meat in frozen and use canned goods, so think convenience, convenience, convenience. You can keep canned items in your pantry and the meat in the freezer and no one will notice how long you've had these items in stock and it will still taste AMAZING. There's a bunch of different recipes that you can use with your crock pot. This will become your most trusted cooking tool in your kitchen.

Note: I listed the price of each item so you know how much it costs to make this meal. This will serve 4-5 people.

2 cans of green beans	$2
1 can of sliced carrots	$1
5 medium/small potatoes	$2
1 lb. of beef chunks	$4
Stew seasoning packet	$1
Total	**$10**

When using canned vegetables, always pour out the liquid and rinse with water. You can do this right in the can. Just pour out the packing fluid, fill with water, rinse, drain and repeat. Wash your potatoes really well and then cut them up into 1/4 or 1/2 inch chunks (keep the skins on them). Put everything into a crock pot and add canned vegetables (the average can is 12 oz.), 24 oz. of water and set temperature setting on low. 6 hours later, it's DONE!

You can leave it on low for 10 hours without it ruining the taste, so set it before you leave for work and your house will smell like a home when you return. Not kidding, but when you and a woman walk in the door and she takes in these scents (a women's sense of smell is almost twice as sensitive as a man's); she is yours because she will feel at home and safe.

- Make this with biscuits or rolls.
- A bottle of Pinot Noir should impress her enough that you should get (at least) nippage!!!

Baked Chicken Caesar Salad

This is a great meal for a few reasons…it's healthy, it's delicious and it's easy to make. All you need is 3 chicken breasts, 2 bags of Caesar salad mix and a little lemon pepper. You can cook this meal while you're in the shower after work.

Make sure that you pull out your frozen chicken in the morning and put it in your sink or fridge. When you get home from work and she's coming over for dinner, place the thawed chicken into one of your baking pans (right….coated with a lot of cooking spray). Sprinkle some lemon pepper on top of the chicken and bake at 350 degrees for 20-25 minutes.

Okay, you're out of the shower and smelling pretty. Using your big handled mixing bowl put both bags of the salad mix in there and stir thoroughly. Take you chicken out of the oven and cut it up into bite size pieces (using your cutting board). Now toss the chicken into your salad and mix it all up again. DONE!

- Serve this with a cold, cold, cold white wine and ice water.
- It's perfect for a hot summer's night.
- If you must have bread with this meal, do French bread.

Stuffed Bell Peppers

Disclaimer: this is the BEST meal that I make and one of my all time favorites. My mom made this all of the time when I was growing up but much differently than I make it today (don't tell my mom, but I like MY version MUCH better).

You're going to need: 2 large bell peppers (colors don't make a difference in taste), shredded cheddar cheese, Spanish rice (look for a box), chunky salsa and a tube of hot/spicy breakfast sausage. Cut the top off of your peppers. Carve out the middle of the bell pepper and remove everything, including the seeds, from the inside. Rinse the bell peppers inside and out. Fry your sausage and break it apart into small pieces.

After it's cooked, drain the grease and pat dry with a paper towel. Prepare the rice with package directions (many may different). Now for the fun part, mix the meat and rice together with 2 heaping (or 4) tablespoons of salsa. Stuff the mixture into the peppers. Place the peppers upright on a baking pan (did you spray your pan?) and put a tablespoon of cheese on top. Bake at 350 degrees for 10 minutes. DONE!

- This is a meal all by itself...so no side dishes are needed.
- Cold stuffed bell peppers are freaking great the next day!
- You can cut these apart in small pieces and serve with tortilla chips to make the world's greatest nachos.

- Try substituting cheddar cheese with a Mexican cheese blend.

Snow Cream

Every year I'd wait for snow as a boy so that we could make snow cream. This is literally homemade ice cream made from snow and it's freaking unbelievable!

Here are a couple of disclaimers: DON'T make this unless you live in the country or a suburban area that's away from pollution. Also, don't make it out of yellow snow…

To make this frosty treat, you'll need: 2 eggs, 2 cans of condensed milk (Milnot or Borden), 1 cup of sugar, 2 tablespoons of vanilla extract, 1 ½ cups of milk (doesn't matter what kind) and fresh snow. Mix up the above ingredients in your large handled mixing bowl~~s~~. Save the snow for last. DONE!

- Remember, I'm not kidding about using clean snow. Pollution can make anyone really sick so don't chance it.
- This can make a winter evening something that everyone will remember for a long time and I promise, they will ask for it again!

Chicken Parmesan

So you want a meal that tastes good, fills you up, everyone likes and you can pack for lunch the next day? How about some chicken parmesan? Oh it's good stuff and easy to make too.

Here's what you need to make this yummy dish: 2 chicken breasts (you can substitute tenders here), 1 box of spaghetti, 1 jar of Ragu (or another sauce that you like), pinch of garlic salt, parmesan cheese, shredded Provel cheese and olive oil. Put 1 tablespoon of olive oil on each piece of chicken and place in your well coated baking pan. Bake at 350 degrees for 25 minutes. Cut open the largest piece of chicken when the time is up and make sure it is white all the way through. If the largest piece is white then the smaller ones will be too.

While your chicken is baking, boil your spaghetti noodles until cooked to your liking (al dente) and drain using your colander. Rinse your pasta with cold water and put into a large handled bowl. Add a pinch of garlic salt and add a quarter cup of olive oil. Mix to coat the noodles really well.

Also while the chicken is cooking, pour the pasta sauce into a small pan and heat on low until it starts to bubble. When it starts to bubble, mix it thoroughly and remove it from the heat. When the chicken is done, stack in on the plate in this order: Pasta, sauce, chicken, sauce, Provel cheese and parmesan cheese. DONE!

- Awesome with steamed broccoli.
- Tastes great with an Italian or French bread.
- Serve with red wine and ice water.

Cheese Ball

This is an incredible appetizer to take to a party! People will literally wait in line to eat it. I don't advise eating an entire cheese ball alone or it will stop you up like you drank a quart of cement. I have never had one complaint EVER with this dish!

Here's what you need to make it: 5 oz. jar of Blue Rocca cheese, 5 oz. jar of Old English cheese, an 8 oz. package of cream cheese, a small bag of pecan bits and crackers (Wheat Thins, etc.) Put all the cheeses into a mixing bowl and with a fork, mix them together. This will take some time, depending on how soft the cheeses are (or, at least 5 minutes and your forearms will feel like you just had a circle jerk marathon).

After it's mixed thoroughly, put on a plate and with the back of a spoon, mold it into half a ball. Put the pecan bits on top. DONE! Serve with crackers.

- The 2 jars of cheese do not need to be refrigerated.
- The cream cheese is softer than the other cheeses.
- If the cheese ball is going to sit in the refrigerator, it must be covered with plastic wrap or it will dry out.

Okay, I've given you a bunch of meals, snacks, deserts and appetizers. There's one more meal that I want to tell you how to make. If you don't use it, I will actually be really farging disappointed…breakfast. I'm hoping that you had a woman over to stay. Annnnnnd…if you want her to do what she just did to you again, leave her with a good taste in her mouth…okay…THAT was funny. So here are 2 quick breakfast recipes to make sure she comes again and again and again…pun intended.

Simple – Fruit and Yogurt

Cut up a banana. Peel and pull apart an orange. Lay the banana and orange out on a plate and drizzle the banana with honey. Serve with a cup of yogurt (not Pina Colada or Gogurt) and a hot cup of coffee or tea. DONE!

- If she stayed over on a school night, this is a perfect quick breakfast.
- Makes sure it's a fruit yogurt (strawberry, banana, cherry)

Easy (like she was last night) – Southwest Omelet

This is actually something that I eat all the time. It's healthy, tastes good and seems to keep me going for the day. It looks hard to make but it's not. I've only had 1 woman ever object to it; so I kicked her ass to the curb…don't bad mouth my eggs!

Here's what you're going to need for each serving: 2 eggs, chunky salsa and shredded cheese (Mexican). Spray your small frying pan with (you guessed it) cooking spray and put it over a medium flame. Put 2 eggs in a bowl and mix them with a whisk or a fork. Then pour your eggs into your pan. When they start getting hard on the bottom, take a handful of cheese and spread it on top of the eggs. As soon as you're done with that, with a spatula, fold the eggs over in half (so it's the shape of half a moon). After 2 minutes, put the spatula under the eggs and flip them over. After 1 more minute, put it on a plate and take a heaping tablespoon of salsa and put it on top of the eggs. DONE!

- Use salt or pepper (or any kind of seasoning that you like) on the eggs while they are in the pan.
- Use as much salsa as you like (any kind of salsa).
- This is a great dish for tailgating.

10 General Kitchen Tips

1. Keep your knives sharp. Most knife sets come with a knife sharpener. Watch a video on YouTube to learn how to sharpen your knives.
2. Make sure that your chicken and pork is well done when cooking. There should be no pink in either one of them when done. Trust me, if you take a guy that eats nothing but turtle ass 364 days a year raw and then on that 365th day you give him a piece of 'pink' chicken, he will shit so much that he'll think "Man, I could go for some turtle ass about now."
3. I put my pancake syrup in a small bowl (I swipe the ones from local restaurants) and heat it up for about 15 seconds.

4. Unsalted butter tastes totally different from salted butter. Get salted butter or you'll be sorry.
5. NEVER let pasta sauce boil. It's like taking a shower and not washing your Willy. It just isn't done.
6. Clean your kitchen as you go. Seriously, by the time my meal is ready to eat my kitchen is pretty clean. The only hot mess you want is in the bedroom!
7. Buy disposable coffee cups with lids. Good lord, the guy that invented them should win the Nobel peace prize. You can send her on her way with a cup of coffee (and a smile on her face) in the morning and you'll never worry about not getting your favorite cup with the Cardinals logo back.

8. Keep apples separate from the rest of your fruit. Apples give off something that will spoil the other fruits.
9. Always keep popcorn in your kitchen. Women LOVE popcorn. Let them salt it but don't give up the remote.
10. I'm big on leftovers. Make sure that you have Tupperware to store food in. It costs much less to make a meal at home and take it for lunch the next day than to eat out.

So now you have some simple dishes that will make you look like an apron wearing Superman.

Just remember a few things:

- Women and men's taste buds are very different. Women can taste the difference in 15 different kinds of dark chocolate and they actually like cucumber sandwiches. Do you know a straight guy that actually like cucumber sandwiches? (Apologies in advance for the one guy that reads this book and works at a cucumber sandwich factory).
- In my experience, most women are foodies (at least 75%). Heavy set women are generally NOT foodies. A foodie is a person that appreciates the taste of certain types of foods together without feeling the need to eat all of their favorite foods until they are stuffed. Heavy set women (IN MY OPINION) simply

eat their emotions…that doesn't make them foodies, it makes them fatties.

- Make all of these dishes for your buddies first. They'll eat it and tell you if it tastes like shit. A woman won't. Plus, it helps you to practice so you actually know what you're doing.
- For a woman, half the pleasure of her meal is the presentation. Not kidding. It has to look good, not simply taste good. My buddy makes a great goulash but you'd never hear a woman say, "Gosh, that was the best goulash I've ever had." My daughter and I had dinner last week. I made some biscuits with my beef stew. I purchased these generic biscuits when she was with me for just 40 cents a can! So I made them and they tasted just okay but they looked unappealing. Naturally, she complained about

them. The next night, we had leftovers. I made the second can of biscuits but this time, I wadded them up like balls before I baked them. I told her that they were drop biscuits and she loved them…..so it's true….make your food pretty.

- Give a lady a child sized portion…I don't know why but just do it.
- Lastly, I hope that I've lit a fire inside of you for cooking. It's easy and can be fun to do. It's healthier and can bring 2 people or even a family together.

Let me know any other recipes that you might have and I may include them (with credit to you) in my next cookbook or post them on my website: divorced-men.com.

Also, remember that you're not alone in this even if sometimes you think you are.

Getting Ready to Date (and the Rating System)

I've heard so many married guys talk about how dumpy their wives look. They see me with an attractive woman and it looks exciting to them. Now, 2 things: most of the time, they're right…their wives do look dumpy. And secondly, I find myself wondering what other woman they could get to actually have sex with them.

I don't want to be mean but I do want to be brutally honest. Let me repeat that…BRUTALLY HONEST. You first have to take a look at yourself and be your own judge. If you look like 230 pounds of chewed bubblegum with your shirt off, if you have been wearing the same clothes for 10 years, if you have yellow teeth and if you have cheesy facial hair while it's patchy on top of your head…what do you expect?

My point is this…how you look and act will determine what kind of woman (women) you can get to have sex with you. So on a scale of 1-10, what are you? Okay, I'll use myself as an example:

- 6 foot tall
- 190 pounds and muscular
- Black hair with some gray (thinning bald spot)
- Don't drive a cool car
- Straight white teeth
- Good skin
- Don't always dress well
- Old phone

- 3 kids
- Very funny and entertaining
- Good listener but sometimes too talkative
- Not a lot of free time
- Poor financially
- Works a lot of hours
- 45 years old
- Showing some wrinkles on my face

How would you score me? I'm a solid 7. That's it. So am I going to get laid by 29 year old, 10's? No. I hang in the 7-8 range and get laid all of the time. In fact, I have much more sex than I should. My point is this: You won't hit any home runs if you're playing basketball…play in your own field (where you should) and you will score. You will get laid.

Find you strengths! Are you funny? Do you like to exercise? Are you a movie buff? Do you like to cook (like me)? Are you a biker (motorcycle)? Do you enjoy ballroom dancing? I can go on but I know you understand…there are women out there that enjoy all of these things and they're looking for a man right now…I'm not kidding!

So you don't have much of a personality? Can't carry a conversation? Don't know what to say around women? Then try having a date at a comedy club!!! The comic's act will give you plenty to talk about afterwards. Laughter is an aphrodisiac and will help you get lucky. Remember that it doesn't really matter what kind of skills or strengths or interests you have…play on your home field and you will score.

Ask yourself this…what kind of women do you want to have sex with? I hope a 'willing' one was your first answer! But aside from that, know in your heart that women are rating you…judging you. With that said, think of this: "Judge not lest ye be judged." So if they are judging you (and they are!) then turnabout is fair play.

You see how I rated myself. I can't rate you without knowing you but you can. I'm a 7. So here's what a 7 is to me in a woman:

- Fun to be around
- Nice body (firm)
- Pretty face
- Nice car
- Good job (not great)

- Clean house
- 32-44 years old (my age)
- Maybe a child or two

So what's an 8 to me? Maybe the above things and a smoking hot body coupled with a woman that's awesome in bed. OR a gal with an amazing job that gets free tickets to everything. OR a woman with a lot of cute friends for my buddies and is rich. See where I'm going with this? Now I'm going to share with you my ratings system that I use:

Note: I start everyone off as a 4 then I either add or subtract based on what these points are worth.

-1.5	3 or more children
-1	2 children
Even	1 child (if you like kids)

+1	great body
+1	incredible face
+ .5	great job
-1	poor financially
-41	alcoholic (don't walk, RUN!)
+1	good sense of humor
+1	cool (you know what I mean)
+.5	similar interest
+1	rich
+1.5	great in bed
+1	dresses sexy
-2	is a slut
+.5	likes PDA
+.25	is a cuddlier
+.5	great laugh
+1	actually eats
+.5	is athletic

+1	good teeth (I actually won't see a women if she has bad teeth)
+1	good skin
-1	bad skin
+1	good cook
-.5	bad cook (I can cook)
+.5	lots of cute friends
+.5	lots of connections
+1	social (fun)
+.5	free tickets to stuff
+1	smells good
+1	feels good
+1	is supportive and encouraging
+.5	is musically talented
+.5	has a clean house
-1	has a dirty house
-2	doesn't believe in God

+1 has that something special that only you can see]

So is my system perfect? No, but it does work for me. Remember with my system, I don't list everything…for example: I listed ½ point plus for a woman that is musically talented but I didn't take a deduction off for her not having any musical talent. Your list of things to take off points for and awarding points has to be as unique as you are. Say you want a woman whose first language is English. That's your choice. You'll never hear me bitching at you about that. Words of advice…keep your list to yourself…forever!!!

Part of getting ready means getting healthy. Chances are you're going to mourn the loss of your relationship (marriage) for a month to 6 weeks. You can use that time to mope around and grieve or you can use that time to get started on looking better.

Let's start on the outside:

- Start by buying a tooth paste that whitens your teeth and use it as directed. In just 6 short weeks, your teeth will be looking brighter.
- If you have body odor (BO), use a cotton swab with rubbing alcohol under your arms to kill the fungus. Do it at night before bed.
- Trim that freaking hair…nose, arms, neck, ears, back and even on your pecker. Chicks don't want to go down on you if they have to cut through a hedge to get there.

- Start eating right…go to bed hungry. Have a big glass of ice water and an apple before bed instead of a beer and chips.
- Don't drink beer unless you're out with people or have people over. You'll be shocked at how much weight you can lose by simply cutting out the suds.
- If you're not exercising now, start. If you haven't worked out in a while, start slowly. It does no good whatsoever to be so sore that you can't/won't work out again. Walk, walk, walk…up stairs and park your car far away in a parking lot. Move your ass.
- Don't cut your hair the same way you have been. Use these 6 weeks to let it grow out and then go to a stylist and ask for a cut that they think will make you look the best. Ask them

how you can make it look like that all of the time (assuming you like it).

- Lose the facial hair…
- Groom, groom, groom…manicure.
- Do kegel exercises daily. You do kegel exercises to help you control how quickly you ejaculate. Other benefits from doing them include increased prostrate health and fuller erections. If you've never heard of kegel exercises for me don't be surprised because most guys haven't. Doing a kegel exercise is simple. When you're urinating stop the stream. That's a kegel exercise. Don't do it only while you're urinating but use those same muscles while sitting on the couch/driving/talking to her on the phone, you get the idea. Flex them and

release. Do 3 sets of 15 of them twice a day. You'll love the results and so will the ladies.

- The last thing I do and the most important thing I did to change myself is this…pushups! I do 150 pushups a day. Pushups will work your arms, core, and shoulders…and it gives you stamina. I do 3 sets of 50. Start off slowly! I repeat…start off slowly! Try by doing 20 pushups a day for 7 days in a row, 2 sets of 10 or 4 sets of 5 and work your way up from there.

The things I've listed in this chapter should do one major thing for you. The one thing that women want more than anything else; women want confidence in a man. Don't be afraid to take charge. Make plans for the evening on your own to show her that you have thought out how you want to spend your time with her. Women eat that shit up! That's it. That's what this chapter is all about. What is on the inside of you will follow when you're overflowing with confidence. Look good first.

So let's go over the highlights again:

1. Rate yourself honestly.
2. Put together your private rating system on what you want a woman to be like.
3. Look for women in your range.
4. Play to your strengths.
5. Respect the grieving process but move on.
6. Do what you need to do on the outside to get ready physically.
7. What do all women really want? Confidence.

Remember that you're not alone in this even if sometimes you think you are.

INEXPENSIVE DATING IDEAS

Most guys never say, "Man, I wish I could spend more money on dates." Let's face it, when you're first separated or recently divorced, you're broke most of the time. You end up supporting 2 households for a prolonged period of time, pay for deposits on utilities, movers, attorney's fees, etc. So when you do start dating again, it's kind of hard to throw away money when you don't have it.

Women don't care about the money (most of them). What they really want is your undivided attention and a little fun (and romance). Earlier I wrote this but I'm going to write it again…don't get caught in the 'friend' trap. If you've gone out with a woman for 10 dates and haven't had sex...then don't plan on having sex with her as you have become their gay friend.

I've been told by women and I've heard through other channels that a woman knows if she's going to sleep with you within the first hour of meeting you. They generally will wait a few dates to have sex with you so they can protect their reputation or save face, socially. So with that in mind, we need to change the mission for our first few dates with them….don't screw it up. Here's the deal. She's going out with you so she can validate wanting to sleep with you. Your job is to keep your conversations and dates lighthearted and fun. Don't have any serious talks from your end. JUST LISTEN.

Men are problem solvers. A woman tells you her problems and a guy thinks that what she's wanting him is to tell her what to do. THEY'RE NOT! They simply want to vent. I know it's tough, but keep your mouth shut and just listen.

Learn the 3 magic words that I've found will get you through many conversations with women (and teenagers). COOL, WOW and BUMMER.

Okay, enough background. Here are several ideas to let her know how special she is to you so she doesn't feel guilty about immediately getting naked with you. All of these ideas will cost less than $40. Many are free (that's right, no cost to you the consumer).

#1 – Themed DVD Night ($20)

This is a great evening with a woman. They will appreciate the fact that YOU put sooo much thought into planning something as simple as a movie with them. But that's not all. Here's a disclaimer: Don't use this date idea with the same woman more than 3 times a year or it will quickly get old and she'll discover that you're really just being a cheap pig.

So grab a DVD and make it a themed evening. What do I mean by that? Well, I've written out some suggestions for you. They include the movie title, food and clothing (optional).

- ANIMAL HOUSE: Yes, one of a guy's all-time favorites. Haul over a six pack of beer, a pizza and a sheet (toga style) for you and her to wear during the movie. When the songs play during the movie get off the couch with her and dance. I bet she'll slip off the toga by the end of the night.

- GODZILLA: Pick any one of the movies (aren't they all the same)? Even though Godzilla is Japanese, bring over Chinese food (or even better, cook to score even more points).

So now you have 2 movies. These should give you ideas for more themed nights. Realize that the movie isn't the attraction of the night. She is. Have a conversation with her. If you need a topic to discuss, you can Google trivia about the movie. Like do you know Kevin Bacon is in the movie, Animal House?

Try to spot him. His big movie line is, “Thank you sir. May I have another?”

Here is what you need to know:

- You can watch the same movie with different women.
- Don’t, don’t, don’t do this for a first date.
- Try to stick with comedies or old horror movies. No slasher/gory or serious flicks. Stick with comedies.
- If you’re watching a movie set in the 50’s, ask something like “Do you want to neck?” If the movie is set in the 60’s, say something like “You’re a groovy chick!”
- The cornier the better on these nights. They will eat it up.

#2 – Ice Skating or Roller Skating ($25)

Most areas have an ice or roller skating rink. Remember how we all skated as kids and had fun? She'll love revisiting this time in her life with you. It can be a fun date that shows you have a playful kid's side to your personality. Be sure to tell her what you're doing in advance. If she has a bad knee, you don't want to find out about it at the skating rink and then be stuck with not having a fun date planned for her. Plus, she'll want to dress appropriately.

Even if you're a bad skater this is a winner of a date with a woman. There's lots of body contact and movement to music. And, this gives you an idea of 'how' she moves. Be fun. Be hokey. Be corny.

- If you fall (be sure to do it on purpose) don't immediately jump right up. Laugh and show her that you're comfortable laughing at yourself.
- Do the couple's skate and east side/west side skates.
- When you take a break, get 1 soda and 2 straws.
- Ask her random questions: Do you come here often? Did you skate as a kid? What was your first boyfriend's name? Did he take you skating? What do you think he looks like now?

#3 – Picnic ($40)

I made the price for this date at the top of our $40 limit for inexpensive dates simply because you want to have good food. She'll think that you are a cheap son of a bitch if you tell her that you're taking her on a picnic. The high quality food will offset those thoughts. She WILL notice your attention to detail. Women are, if anything, observant.

Here are the rules:

- Have a big CLEAN blanket. Don't pull out the one you've had in the trunk of your car for a year.
- Have 2 good bottles of wine.
- Bring fruit and cheese.

- Ask for help at the grocery store/deli if you're not comfortable with the food selection.
- Bring something to do (cards, bocce ball, Frisbee, dominoes or part of your favorite book.

Remember that this isn't just about the menu. She will notice the quality of the food that you packed. This is about ~~a~~ good conversation with her. Make her feel special. Make her feel comfortable with you. Make her feel safe and she'll do her best to make you feel good.

#4 – Bike Ride (Free to $10)

I'm assuming that you both own bikes. If not, then go for a walk in the park. If you both decide to go bike riding, look for an easy ride where you can pedal and talk, without paying too much attention to operating your bike (a trail is perfect for this).

I listed $10 as the cost so you could buy her an ice cream or a soda after the ride. Remember to bring water for both of you. This is a shorter date (unless she's a fitness chick). So plan on an hour or two at most.

- Sorry, she's probably not going to want to get naked after this but if she does, you both can grab a shower together.

- This is a groundwork date for you. It's actually a perfect 1st date.
- If you're going for a walk, hold her hand. Women feel a real physical connection holding hands and respond to human touch as long as they feel safe doing it. Holding hands shows them that you are respectful.

#5 – Grocery Shopping (Free, you need food)

I know that shopping sounds more like a chore but if you're learning anything from this book, then you know it doesn't really matter what you do as long as #1) She feels safe and #2) You do it with confidence. Grocery shopping can not only be engaging but it can be romantic as well. Try going to a farmer's market. Smell the fresh produce with her (lemons, limes, apples and oranges). Women's sense of smell is much more acute than a man's so engage their olfactory (this is also why I will tell you to wear aftershave/body spray/cologne, at all times). Sample the grapes and other fresh fruits. Hold up carrots like rabbit ears and say, "What's up, Doc?"

Remember that I told you that from my experience, 75% of women are foodies. Well brother, here is where it starts…impress them with your meal planning and they will throw their panties at you. I know this because they throw their panties at me.

Many larger grocery stores offer cooking classes or wine tastings for free or for a small charge.

- This is an ideal Saturday morning date (then you both can spend the afternoon under the covers).
- This is also an easy way to spend a winter's afternoon (at a big indoor store). When you take her back to unload your groceries, you can unload something else too!
- This is a great second or third date. She can see you in a domestic setting and think what it will

be like to have a relationship with you. You can use that to explore what kind of a lover she is (insert wink here).

- I've been laid so many times using this date idea that I promise you, it works!

#6 – Cup of Coffee ($5-10)

Let me start by saying, this is ALWAYS my 'go-to' 1st date. I do this for 2 simple reasons…1) I will see if I'm interested in her. 2) If she's a pig, then I can slam my coffee down and get the heck out of there with very little time or money invested. I ALWAYS meet them for coffee if I meet them on a dating website.

Now, let's assume that they aren't a pig and then do the following things:

- Turn you phone off.
- Look into her eyes.
- Ask her question and then LISTEN to her answers before you respond.

- Dress business casual (even if it's a Saturday and it's 100 degrees outside).
- Lead with the words "tell me about…" it shows confidence that you are interested in and expect an answer. Tell me about…your mom and dad, your brothers and sisters, kids, best friend (how did you meet?), job (what do you like/hate?), pets, etc.
- Don't ask them about their ex or past relationships!!!
- Women WANT/DESIRE/NEED to talk about themselves….so….let them.

#7 – Clothes Shopping (Free to ?)

I'm all over the board on how much this will cost you. That's because I've got a buddy and this is his 'go to' move. He scores with women well out of his range with this move on a regular basis and it doesn't cost him much at all. Why? Because he returns the clothes they pick out for him for a full refund!!!

Here's how it works: "Julia, I was wondering if you could help me? You know that I'm single and don't really have anyone to help me with this. I really admire your style. You seem so stylish and know what looks good. Would you mind helping me shop for some clothes?" Guess what? He's almost never turned down. He gets to spend 3 hours with a totally, hot woman that he lets pick out clothes for him and see if they fit right. She gets to see him do what she tells him to do (women like that). They get to laugh and joke around and then he INSISTS on taking them out to dinner to THANK them. AND get this…if he doesn't score (about a 25% success rate) then he asks them to set him up with a hot girlfriend!

- This is a way for you to go well above your rating level and get a woman 2-3 points above, where you actually are.
- My friend is a 6 and he has scored with a couple of 9's doing this.
- If you return the clothes, it doesn't cost you anything…except the cost of dinner with an attractive woman.
- It's awesome to take photos of the two of you shopping and post them on Facebook. (It

makes other women that you know think, "what am I missing out on with him?)

- If she sets him up with one of her ~~a~~ girlfriend's then it introduces him to a new group of women.

Okay…I don't do this. I never have. I honestly get enough action my own way that I don't have to scam women. I love his thoughts and ideas that he's put into this though.

#8 – Fire ($15)

So why does a fire cost $15 is the question I'd be asking, if I were you. Because I'm going to give you a magic recipe that has NEVER failed to get me laid. It has to be chilly outside to use this method so from May-August, it's a no go but otherwise…it's golden! So why do I call it a recipe? It literally is a recipe. I make a homemade mulled wine that I'm now going to share with you; before I do, promise yourself to NEVER share with her how to make this.

Get a bottle of cheap white wine (chardonnay), cinnamon sticks, whole cloves and a heaping cup of sugar. Put all of this into a pot, PLUS fill up the wine bottle ¾ of the way with cold water and put into the pot too. Heat it on the stove until it comes to a fast boil and then serve it hot in coffee mugs. After a woman drinks 2 cups of this, YOU will be their favorite guy of all time. This has NEVER failed me.

- Just sit outside and chat while you both enjoy some of this.
- Sit by a fireplace.
- This is a great 3rd date idea. She's thinking about it anyway…

#9 – Christmas Lights (Free- $20)

From Thanksgiving until New Year's, there are a ton of Christmas lights all over the city; from private displays to public displays. Take a drive and get your holiday groove on…

Load a thermos full of hot chocolate (with Bailey's), hot apple cider or my mulled wine recipe in #8 and let the spirit of Christmas surround you both. Maybe she'll feel good enough to give you a present early…

- Bring a holiday music CD (try 'George Winston-December' or 'GRP Christmas').
- Tell her a story about how Christmas was for you growing up.
- Ask her what her favorite toy was that she got as a little girl for Christmas.

#10 – Zoo ($10-30)

Most metropolitan areas have a zoo. In my hometown, the zoo is actually free to enter; whereas most cities have a small entrance fee. Go for a walk around the zoo and look at the animals. Hold her hand. Share a bag of popcorn. Sit and talk (it all goes back to that).

Be sure to buy her a balloon and make her tie it to her wrist. See her favorite animal. Ask her why she likes them. Bottom line…show her a good time and then take her home and show her who the real King of the jungle really is!!!

#11 – A Party (Free)

Almost everyone knows someone that is having a party. Take her as your date. It's really that simple. It has some pitfalls so be warned but it's a cheap way for you both to go out and have some fun together. Here are the pros and cons:

- There will always be an asshole there that will bring up you and your ex, so be ready to respond.
- She will get to see you with your friends and will actually picture herself as part of your social circle.
- If you take out a lot of women, someone (generally a friend's wife) will tell her all about it.

- It's a great icebreaker and awesome as a 2nd or 3rd date.
- It will often get you over the hump if you haven't had sex with her yet.

#12 – Shakespeare ($40)

Most metro areas present Shakespeare festivals each year. Many of these productions are called 'Shakespeare in the Park." They are free plays given by amateur actors. Don't expect high quality anything ~~in~~ from these plays but you get what you pay for in this case (or don't pay for). I listed $40 for the same reasons as I did for the picnic. This is basically the same date idea but instead of you, bringing the entertainment, the play is the main feature and is generally, at night.

Bring some citronella candles along with a basket full of light goodies for you both to nibble on. I will usually Google the play or bring some cliff notes along and openly read them to her. They love that last move!!!

Just remember, as always, keep it lighthearted and maybe you can do your own, "Taming of the Shrew."

- Try fruit and cheese with a nice sweet white wine.
- Cold beer and hot pretzels with spicy mustard.
- You can even bring along a pizza from a local place.
- Be unique and different.

#13 – Home Depot (Free)

Who knew being a man could pay off by taking a woman to a hardware store and getting her to play with your hammer? Well, it can. The big store chains often offer classes on how to put up decorative tile and learn faux painting. Women love doing this stuff; yet are often intimidated and don't want to go alone. I'll be honest with you…I'm very good at home repair and remodeling but I still take women to these classes.

They think that it's great that I take them and can actually teach them a few "other" tricks (pun intended). I watch shows on networks like HGTV and the DIY network all the time so I know the lingo. Say things like 'creating a comfortable living space is important.' Or 'you'll need a quality piece to make the room pop.' Or 'color coordination from room to room will help the flow.' Now if they don't think you're gay, then be prepared to have her panties actually hit you in the face because they literally will.

I once had a hot, steamy afternoon with a beautiful lady physician by showing her how to wire some electrical outlets! Women are turned on by men who not only have these skills but are willing to teach them how to do it. Secretly, a woman desires a man that can take care of her. A woman's living space is like a piece of her body. Most guys don't pay attention to it and she won't give them the time of day. Don't be that guy.

- IMPORTANT: Don't do a lot of repairs around a woman's house if she's not doing a lot for you (in the bedroom or anywhere else). If you do, you will be her "special friend" but not her sex partner.

- Watch HGTV and simply repeat the key terms they use.
- Say things to her like, "I'd like to see you wearing my tool belt and nothing else…" then laugh like crazy! She'll get the hint and then it's in her mind.
- Remember, women love a guy that can fix things.

#14 – Pizza ($30)

There aren't many people out there that don't like pizza and beer. Go to a local place (stay away from pizza chains) and order a specialty pizza and a pitcher of suds. Now here's the trick…don't be in a hurry. This evening isn't about the food or the drink (at least for women). This is time for you to get to know each other. So be laid back and fun.

Tell her you will let her order the pizza if you get to pick the beer. She'll agree to that in a heartbeat. If she doesn't drink beer then this will be a long ass evening….not kidding. Let her order what she wants and then get what you want to drink. Let her talk and then see where it leads.

This evening is simply about getting her to open up, so remember:

- Ask open- ended questions (I always just say, 'Tell me…'). Say, "What's your dad like?" instead of "Do you have a good relationship with your dad?"
- Don't be in a hurry and don't rush the food or the drinks.
- If you go to a place that has a ton of kids or loud music then you're screwed. Scout it out first. I have a go-to place for this date.

#15 – Bonfire (Free)

If you're living in a heavy urban area then it might not help you to read this idea. I live in a suburban area and have a fire pit. I get a lot of use out of that little bastard. What a great $69 investment!

Start a fire and crack open a bottle of wine. You set out a couple of lawn chairs and relax. I actually have a double chair by my fire pit so she has to sit next to me. I often make my 'mulled wine' that I gave you the recipe for earlier and end up getting my pole waxed.

- Make sure you have the wood (to burn).
- Make sure the weather is going to cooperate.

- If you're making dinner, try making small sandwiches cut into quarters. Use paper plates that you can just throw in the fire.
- I have a story that I always tell about Native Americans and their belief in the purity of sitting fireside. Find your own story about fire and share it.
- Be sure to practice telling your story (like you'd rehearse a sales pitch) that way you're more animated when with her.

#16 – Drive in the Country ($40)

I listed the price high because fuel is so damned high right now. Plan on bringing some snacks (cheese and crackers, fruit and water). Women love seeing nature (as long as it's clean). Drive by a farm and look at the cows, horses and sheep. Enjoy the leaves falling or the corn coming up. Look for deer and hawks. Stop at an old church and look at the headstones. If you can stop for homemade jelly or wine at a roadside stand then definitely do it.

This is a great first or second date where you can let her talk all day. Remember that's what women like to do. Bring along a jazz CD.

- Remember the journey IS the destination on this date.

- Never bitch about traffic or other people's driving.
- Take your time.
- Make sure your car is clean.
- Hold her hand. Let her know that you think of her as yours (they love it).

#17 – Jazz Club ($40)

Almost every place in the U.S. has a jazz club. I've seen towns that only have 2,000 people in them and even they have jazz bars or piano bars. These are great places to go on dates because they are uber cool. You can sit back and look at the lady you brought with you. She's wearing a killer outfit and you're wearing a nice pair of slacks and a nice shirt (long sleeve buttoned down). Your shined shoes are tapping to the beat of the music and you can sip on a few mixed drinks and enjoy the evening.

- —When the music is playing, keep the conversation is at a minimum.
- Hold her hand and let the bar (including her) know that she's with you.
- Wear aftershave or cologne.

- Pull your chair on the same side as her so you can both look at the stage (and it gives you better body contact).
- Your value (in her eyes) just went up a point to a point in a half.

#18 – BBQ ($40)

This is a win/win/win date. First, because you get to stay home and grill some manly meat and drink beer with your buddies. Secondly, because she gets a feel for who you are and why your friends like you. And lastly, because it will make her feel like a couple and you will be rewarded with sex! It all comes back to getting rewarded, right? So, enjoy it. I listed $40 because you're going to buy meat, sauce and beer. Ask your friends to bring the rest (sides, bread, ice, bottled water or soda).

Here's a quick trick for your sauce: Melt a stick of butter into your favorite BBQ sauce (I like Sweet Baby Rays).

- Have some games on hand (horse shoes, bocce ball, etc.)
- If there's a game on soooo much the better.
- Make sure that you introduce her to everyone there and mention what they might have in common.

#19 – Haunted House ($40)

Most places in the Midwest have haunted houses from October 1st thru the first weekend in November. Tickets aren't cheap. Many offer discounts if you buy them and print them off from your own computer. Look for coupons. Another way to save money is to look for a Groupon.

This is a fun evening out. Have a couple of drinks with her and then take her there. She will LOVE screaming and acting like a little girl all while you're the brave man who laughs in the face of danger (or in this case, high school kids dressed as zombies).

- Even if she wets herself, be sure to compliment her on how brave she was.

- Hang around afterwards and watch people come out of the haunted house. You can laugh at how they are acting.
- Make sure she's okay with going BEFORE you buy the tickets.

#20 – Cook a Meal Together ($40)

You're an expert by now, right? Women love doing this because they want to see if you're going to be a helpful mate. Trust me, they ARE judging you. So why not take the bull by the horns and show off your culinary skills. 9 times out of 10, I got laid by simply inviting a woman over for a meal and then cooking for her.

- Know what you're going to make and have everything ready to cook…be prepared.
- Make sure your house is picked up (especially, the bedroom).
- Have a couple of bottles of wine on hand (sometimes we have to give them an excuse to sleep with us…so if it's a mistake, they can say

to their friends ‘I had too much wine that night.’)

- Think candles (in the bedroom too, especially if they’re gonna want the lights off.)
- Make your food look pretty.
- If a woman tells you NO when you ask her, what she’s really saying is ‘I’m not ready yet.’

#21 – Balloon Release ($40)

This is a date that she will tell her friends about. This is a sure fire get laid date!!! Use it sparingly. Word will get out quickly so if you do this to 3 or 4 women, they will know that you're just using it to get laid (then its goodnight and not in the good way).

Here's the gist of the date: Women love symbolism, they freaking live for that crap. So give it to them. You're going to need 10 helium balloons, string, a magic marker and index cards. I'd bring along a blanket and a bottle of wine. Tell her that you are both going to let go of 5 negative things in your lives. After you write on the index cards, tie them to the balloons and let them go. Pray that she's not giving up casual sex!

Take your time with writing things out on your cards. She will. Don't worry or panic though because I'm going to give you some things to put down on your cards that will make you look like a thoughtful and insightful man. REGRET, ANGER, SADNESS, LETHARGY and SOCIETY'S VIEW OF PERFECTION. Put those 5 down and her legs will open up.

- This is a home run date. If a woman doesn't sleep with you after this date it is because it's her time of the month.
- Take your time when you're writing these down and be prepared to hear several stories from her. How you react will depend on what happens next.

- Don't do this on a first date! This is a 3rd date or later, if she's not putting out. This will get her over the hump.
- Hopefully, the weather cooperates with you. If it doesn't, don't push the situation. If it's 30 degrees out and raining, it will suck.
- You can either buy the balloons filled up or buy a kit from a store that will have a small helium tank.

So I've given you some really good dates that won't break the bank. Here are the highlights of this chapter:

1. Dating doesn't have to be expensive.
2. Women love creative dates because it shows you're thinking about them.

3. Keep the date about them. Don't check out other women and let them talk about themselves.
4. Don't use this big date idea on every woman.

Remember, you're not alone in this even if sometimes you think you are.

HOW TO GET LAID

So now we've come to the chapter that gets most people worked up (pun, not intended). This is the chapter that most guys want to read first. I will advise you to NOT get caught up with sex. Sex is easy to get. I've had lots of sex with a lot of different women from all walks of life. I've always been blessed/cursed with this ability. Blessed for the obvious reason…cursed because I didn't love these women, except for my wife. Sex cost me that relationship (coupled with pride) and me and my family suffered for it. Sex – when you love someone is so very much better than just sex by itself.

Okay, you've read the disclaimer. So read on if you're interested in getting laid.

Getting laid is work! However, the reward is sex so it's a great payoff! The good news is that you don't have to go to clubs or bars every night to get laid. Bad news is that you do have to get your fat ass off of the couch and away from your TV. So, without bars or clubs? Where to then?

Try some of these places:

- Coffee shops
- Gym
- Classes
- Grocery store
- Church (not kidding)
- Volunteer groups
- Social meet up groups
- Outdoor concerts

- Dating sites (I'll give you a lot on this in a bit)

We've talked earlier about what kind of woman you should go after. We also covered the subject on how you look and how you rate. So when you go out, look for the woman that's in your sweet spot (your ratings equal). The hardest thing to do when you are getting laid is starting up a conversation with a woman. You have to be unique. You don't go up to a woman in a bar and say, "So do you like Star Wars or Star Trek better?" Unless you're at Comicon, you're done. Don't say, "You've got a great smile." either. They don't want to hear cheese ball compliments about their looks.

You're better off walking up to them (looking at them in the eyes) and saying, "Excuse me, but you're in my spot." She'll be confused and say, "What?" Start laughing and then say, "Kidding, forgive me but I don't have any pickup lines and it's all I could think of to start a conversation with you." Now shut up! If she says something else, offer to buy her a drink and continue the conversation. If she looks around awkwardly, she's not interested…save your money and don't buy her a drink.

Remember this book (me) wants you to be happy. Getting laid and being happy is all about confidence. If you want to get laid when you talk to a woman – speak, stand and act with confidence. That's what a woman finds the sexiest in a man…confidence. Men and women think of sex with total different expectations. For most men, it's a physical function. For women, it's a spiritual thing. I once heard a comedian say "Women need a reason to have sex while men just need a place to have sex." In short, this guy (no idea who it was) was right.

Guys listen to me…what I'm about to write next is the most important line in this entire book…WOMEN NEED A REASON TO HAVE SEX. They need to justify sleeping with you. So make sure that you give them a reason to have sex with you. Most of the time (if you don't screw up in the first few dates) is enough of a reason for them. It's called "reasonable time sex." It's very real and they (many times) abide by it. If they go out with you 3 times, it's a signal that they are ready. So if you look at it that way…think…cook for them on the 3rd date. You're at home. It's quiet. You're alone. If she comes, chances are good that she wants it too. Think ahead. Put yourself in a position to succeed.

Since guys pay more attention to bullet points, the rest of this chapter is listed as bullets. Learn it…know it…live it.

Here are a few tips/rules/guidelines to getting laid:

- You will NEVER get laid when a woman is with a group of her friends. So don't try (they don't want a guy who failed). Just be fun and she will want to be alone with you.
- Coffee is the best first date. If she's great, you will know and if she's a freak then you can get the hell out of Dodge and it just cost you a cup of coffee.

- Fooling around with a woman is one thing but once you put the ‘P’ in the ‘V’, it changes the rules. She’ll claim you as hers.
- After shave and body spray go a long way…smell good.
- NEVER check out another woman when on a date. Even if she’s in the bathroom, she will know.
- Never check out your date’s cleavage. She’s putting it out there for you as a test. Don’t fall for it.
- Unless she leaves her purse in your car, don’t call her for 24 hours! YES it’s a fucking rule! She won’t find it cute (even if she says it). She’ll think that you’re a needy pussy so don’t do it. If you text her the next day, keep it short.

Text something like "Had a great time at dinner. Let's do it again next Thursday."

- I found out that nice guys don't get laid! I said it. I'm not saying be a dick to them but if you're overly friendly then she will not respect you like you think. Hey it's not the 1950's.
- Don't offer to fix stuff at their house or offer to loan them money.
- If a woman uses sex as a weapon, get the fuck out of there. I don't care if she gives the best head ever.
- Don't try to cure an alcoholic. Don't walk away. RUN away! It's not your responsibility to care for her. I was suckered into a 2 year relationship because I felt I HAD to be there or I'd be abandoning her. I was an idiot. Fuck that and don't do it.

- I like low maintenance women. If you want to be in an exclusive relationship with them, tell them.
- Don't share your health issues with them until you're engaged to them. Trust me they don't want to know.
- Stay away from talking about money with a woman as long as possible. If she asks, be vague and say something like, "I do alright."
- Don't talk about other women that you've dated. If you say something stupid like, "My ex-girlfriend really loved this restaurant too," then you're a freaking idiot and deserve to spank your own monkey.
- NEVER EVER complain about your ex. Here's how women see it (and we should too)…if you talk poorly about your ex then you

may (someday) say the same negative shit about them too.

- Sex is easy to get. Don't forget it.
- Don't send her flowers until after you've nailed her or you will always be the pathetic guy.
- A movie is a rotten first date. Go someplace that you can talk.
- Try lotion on your face after you shave…NO beard burn. The rough look is in right now but if you're planning some alone time then shave clean. If you're going down on her or plan on making out with her, do her a favor and shave.
- In the beginning of the relationship, avoid chain places to eat. Tell her that you want to take her to places as unique as she is.

- Dogs are a great way to meet women but they are a ton of work so I've never personally used them.
- Wine is a great gift to give to a woman.
- Don't bring break every single skeleton out of the closet. I know a lot of guys think that they need to disclose every negative thing in their life and be honest before they sleep with a woman…you know what I call those guys? Masturbators!
- Listen-listen-listen because I swear that she will tell you how to have sex with her. She'll tell you her favorite cologne, food, wine, uncle, movie, music and movie star.
- If a woman has 'daddy issues' find out what kind of after shave her dad wears. Put it on and

she will wrap her legs around your freaking face.

- Dress business casual for your first couple of dates. I don't care if it's at 9 a.m. on a Saturday morning, just do it.
- If you're overly polite to a woman never plan on seeing her naked, homo.
- Always be in a good mood before a date and it will carry over.
- If they cancel the date, don't react negatively other than being understanding. Wait 2-3 days before calling them again. Don't let them think that they are the only game in town.
- Be quick to laugh at yourself if you spill a drink or drop a fork. Women love when a guy does that.

- Laugh-laugh-laugh=sex.
- Don't, for the love of God, tell jokes during your date.
- All women like music so start playing a musical instrument (guitar, for me).
- Don't tell a woman your problems during a date. Therapy is one thing but if you want some naked therapy then shut the hell up.
- Your grandparents (if they're cute and not pigs) are a great way to get laid. Introduce a woman to your grandma and she will give you the goods.
- Turn your ringer off and don't check your phone when out with a woman. If you're expecting a call tell her in advance and say, "I'm sorry but I may have to take a call from

(whomever) that I will need to take during our date. I want to tell you in advance because I don't want you thinking that you don't have my full attention tonight."

- 3-4 dates (5 at most) mean sex. Period. If you're out on your 10th date and nothing has happened, cut your dumb ass losses...she's not into you and an 11th date won't make the difference.
- Many guys that are newly single get a condition called 'rubber rash.' This is because they never wore a condom with their wife but they are now. The head of your penis may dry out. My doctor told me to just take a dab of Vaseline each morning and put it around the head of my penis. Good news...my penis is still working and actually looks years younger.

- Confidence equals sex.

Read this again until it sinks in…not kidding. Wear your game face. Having sex is like doing business….close the deal. Treat it that way. Sex is easy. Don't make it out to be so very difficult. K I S S = keep it simple shithead. Follow these rules and you will get laid.

Now let's talk about Internet dating. I hear this commercial constantly on the radio that states 40% of all relationships begin now online. I don't know if it's true or not, but I've had a ton of success from online dating. I'm a big fan of it because I work a lot. It's great. You get a chance to 'meet' a woman, get to know her a little and talk to her on the phone, all before you have to actually meet them. They will give you plenty of things for you to refer to when you meet them. Things that you can reference when you're meeting them for the first time…"remember when you told me about your grandma?"

Quick tip: Review your emails with her before you meet her. For your Internet profile, make sure that you're completely honest about your situation. If you're separated say it. Don't say divorced. Put up a clear and recent photo of yourself. Have someone else take it. No problem, if you suck in your gut or tilt your head a certain way but otherwise make it all you.

Here's how my profile reads on Match.com:

i write all of the time, but never about myself. oh well, let's give it a try. i mean, i wouldn't want to disappoint my old english teacher. i'm the most creative person that i've ever met, so if you are looking to laugh and like an intellectual challenge, then please read on. my children are very important to me. i'm a soccer dad...it's tough to admit but i am (how did that happen?--lol). i love spending time doing kid stuff. i appreciate who they are at an early age and enjoy aiding them on finding their path to happiness. my 2 oldest daughters are grown. heck, one is married. now i keep my 11 year old with me as much as i possibly can.

if you don't believe in happy endings and romance and love and you're just looking for a fling then STOP reading. i'll save you some time...i'm not the guy for you. if, however, you do believe in love at first site and holding hands and truly being happy from within then hello. here's a little you should know..........

i don't appreciate high maintenance people. i'm definitely not one. think of the word metrosexual. i'm the exact opposite of that. i can laugh and joke about myself and frequently do! i used to perform standup comedy on a regular basis but haven't performed in about 4 years. that's soon going to change...i have a TON of material just from being on match.com...lol....so c'mon and give me some more material!!!

i don't do drama---lol. life is too short and you never get out alive anyway. you might as well have fun.

i don't like people who are late or sloppy (sorry only two hang-ups). I also don't like Cool Ranch Doritos (what were they thinking?)

if you like to laugh and have a good time then don't hesitate to email me. let's see how smart, creative and fun that you really are.

lastly, i often wear my heart on my sleeve. i'm a true believer that people should be and need to be in love. we are better and happier when we are.

i'm looking for a relationship with someone that makes me laugh, likes to be held, is dependable, intelligent, who believes that family is important, believes in God, takes care of themselves, likes MY cooking and likes being social.

i am not looking for a trophy wife/girlfriend. however, i know that couples should find each other attractive so that the initial spark becomes a flame. so if you don't take care of yourself physically then i'm sorry but i'm probably not the guy for you. i want a WOMAN not a girl. someone with real life experience who knows what it's like to be in love and to be loved. i want a life partner (not gay). i want to wake up with the same person for the rest of my life and say 'thank you god for putting this person in my life.' i want someone that wants to hold my hand and that's affectionate and wants to snuggle on the couch or in bed on a cold rainy day.

i hope that this has given you a sense of who i am and what i stand for. i mean, no one can write a paragraph or two and paint an accurate picture of themselves.

i hope the paragraphs that i've written have, a least, given you an idea though.

thanks for taking the time to look.

if i'm not the guy for you, then i wish you good luck on finding happiness.

I simply copied and pasted this from my Match profile. Feel free to copy this to your dating profile or use any part of it that applies to you. I had literally hundreds of emails, winks and a over a thousand views from this. Many of them said "I love cool ranch Doritos." What that told me is that they were following what I wrote so put something unique in yours. Mention anything that sets you apart from the hundred other guys out there.

- Don't say you make $200k if you don't...say 'I do alright.'
- Don't say you're out of shape...say 'health conscience.'
- Don't say you're not a regular church goer...say 'you're spiritual.'

Now I told you earlier not to lie on your profile. I stick to my statement. With that being said, you don't have to tell 100% of the truth either. I know. I know it's a lie by omission but c'mon…you don't have to tell them that you've been to the last 6 Star Trek conventions.

Think of yourself as a used car. You may have some wear and tear. You might have a couple of scratches on the paint and maybe a dent or two but you don't have to point out every little negative thing. You say, look at that interior. It was owned by a nonsmoker and serviced regularly. I'll spell it out for you: "I'm a great guy with a lot to offer. I believe in soul mates. Do you? I'm happy and simply looking to share my life with another person."

Hey, believe those words and you're simply expressing your opinion! Don't go into a dating site thinking that a woman is just flirting with you online. You have to do something to make yourself different. Try getting her talking.

Ask her these eight simple questions:

1. Thick or thin crust?
2. Chocolate or vanilla?
3. Dog or cat?
4. Beach or mountain?
5. Movie or play?
6. Wine or beer?
7. Football or baseball?
8. Winter or summer?

What do these questions tell you when she answers them? It tells me 2 things: It tells me that she's interested in me and it tells me that if I can keep her talking that I have a better chance of seeing her without those cutoff jeans on. Women like to talk about themselves. Always remember that. Keep her talking about herself. Quick tip: If a woman's profile shows photos of just her face, she's probably heavy.

I mentioned Match.com but there are a lot of other sites out there as well and still more coming out all the time, for example:

- Zoosk.com
- Eharmony.com
- Ourtime.com
- Christianmingle.com
- Singleparent.com

- Adultfriendfinder.com
- Chemistry.com
- Pof.com

Explore your options. There's no law that you have to only be on one dating site. Women are all over.

So now you're dating but not really getting anywhere or you've spent the last 20 years with only one woman and you're not sure how to advance to the sex stage again. Hey don't be embarrassed. It doesn't make you a pussy or lessen you in any way in my eyes.

In the chapter, Adjustment, I told you what I do each day and what I do before sales calls. Do those before each date. Here are a few tips to build your confidence in the bedroom:

- Make sure your pubic hair is trimmed back. It really does make your junk look bigger.
- Foreplay, foreplay, foreplay…enough said. Women love it and often need it to reach an orgasm.
- NEVER cum first! Always let her get off first. I don't care how tired or horny you are.
- I know it's uncomfortable but always wear a condom.
- Try using your thumb in her vagina while massaging her ass with your hand.
- Women love having their clitoris stimulated. Take 2 fingers and rub it gently (gently) in a counterclockwise motion.

- Some women lose wetness after a while. It has nothing to do with you. Keep some lubricant handy for their comfort (and yours).
- When performing oral sex on a woman try writing the alphabet with your tongue.
- When performing oral sex on a woman insert your index finger into her and stimulate their G spot. It's on the front of the vaginal wall about an inch up.
- Realize that every sexual encounter is not going to be like a scene from a movie. This is real life.
- There are a ton of sexual positions. Look up an illustrated version of the karma sutra online.
- A friend of mine swears by the saying '2 in the pink and 1 in the stink.' He's referring to

putting 2 fingers into a woman's vagina and 1 finger into her anus. I don't like anal (never have) so I can't vouch for this because I've never tried it.

- Ask her what she likes. Most of the time she'll tell you.

Now many guys will have trouble going from kissing to anything farther at all. I know how that can be. You're scared and a little unsure. You don't want to run her off by scaring her but at the same time you want to do more.

Something that I've done a lot of times (dozens and dozens) and never been called out on is this: When I'm kissing a woman, I put both of my hands on her face or her head then I use my forearms to rub her breast. She's thinking: "My breasts are being stimulated but I'm not ready for that, but wait, both of his hands are on my face so he must not know that he's doing it?" So they keep letting me. They get turned on by this and so when I move my hand over they never object. I think a lot of the times they are so very ready for me to do it that they're squirming for it.

You can also do a casual brush up again them with your hand to see if they are ready. Move your hand up from your waist to their face and touch their breast on the way up. If there's no objection then they want you to do it. Be confident my friend. That's what they want.

Ok…so now you know how to get laid. Understand that this knowledge can change your life. I never worry about having sex. I can't imagine otherwise. I know so many of my friends who would give anything to have this ability.

Now you have all of the knowledge that I have. I hope that you have the same results. I will tell you one last time though that sex with someone that you truly love is beyond measure better than sex with someone that you hardly know. Do you want to review what you've learned in this chapter?

1. Sex is easy.
2. Women love/desire/crave confidence.
3. Nice guys don't get laid.
4. Use the Internet.
5. Women love to talk about themselves so let them.
6. Put yourself in a position to succeed.

Remember, you're not alone in this even if sometimes you think you are.

HOLIDAY SURVIVAL

This has been the toughest chapter of this book for me to write because I struggle with it personally. Let me give you a little background first: Growing up, the holiday season was always very special to me. From Halloween to Thanksgiving to Christmas to New Year's, our house was always filled with friends and family. We never got candy growing up except for that time of year so it was awesome! Not to mention, the turkey and stuffing and Christmas lights and presents and fun.

When I got married and had my own family, those traditions and fun times simply continued. When I was divorced, I seemed to have lost my favorite time of year. I didn't have the kids and the holidays were spent alone or with someone that I didn't really care for.

Realizing that my ex and my children were celebrating the holidays without me made matters worse somehow. It became even harder for me when my ex brought someone new into the picture. This stranger had moved into my chair at the table with my children; that put me into a down place. I realized that my ex-wife wasn't trying to hurt me, she's simply moved on. She's finding her own way and there's nothing wrong with that. I just had to find out how to do that myself.

Have I done that? Let's just say that I'm a work in progress…

Instead of claiming to be an expert in this part on divorced life (and I'm not), I will simply throw out some ideas that I've heard, some things that I've done and what my friends have done that have worked for them to ease the 'sting' of the holidays.

Here are some tips to ease the holiday blues:

- Volunteer to ring a bell for the Salvation Army.
- Go to church a lot.
- Call every member of your family to say 'happy holidays.'
- Go to a family dinner.
- Go to every Christmas party you can.
- Exercise a lot.
- Don't put up a tree (I know I don't need to but I always do).

- Lay off of the booze (curb it back).
- Get involved anywhere you can. Stay busy.
- Avoid watching Christmas specials on TV.
- Avoid Christmas music.
- Eat well and eat healthy. You'll feel better after the holidays if you've dropped a few pounds.
- If you can get away go to the islands or Mexico.
- Get a part time job to make some extra cash.
- Host a party.
- Have friends come over to watch 'A Charlie Brown Christmas.'
- For Halloween, give out candy.
- If you have kids, enjoy the hell out of them!

Quick tip: It's so freaking easy to have sex at this time of year. I'm talking about having multiple partners during this time. Women are so caught up in the holidays and they don't want to be alone for New Year's Eve that it's honestly like shooting fish in a barrel.

In this chapter, I gave you all of my tips in bullet forms so a chapter review is not needed.

Remember, you're not alone in this even if sometimes you think you are. Especially, at this time of year…

Conclusion & Acknowledgements

I'd like to give a special note of thanks for 3 friends without whom I doubt I would have ever finished this book…thanks, Skippy and Scotty. Not only did I live with the 2 of you like brothers but we worked as a team for a while, discussing dating strategies and how to date on a dime because we were always broke. Some of our times were golden and some, I wouldn't mind forgetting. If I never see either one of them in their tightie-whities over breakfast, it will be OKAY with me! We had our good times cooking, swimming, drinking and simply hanging out. I will always treasure my time, at the 'Frat House.'

I'd also like to thank Ms. Lois "Cosby" Francis for rolling her eyes at me every time she thought that I insulted women in this book, for her corrections and edits of this book, but especially for inspiring me to finish writing this book. I love and appreciate her.

Now that the nice things are said, let's get to the conclusion of this book.

Divorce is hard guys; not just on us or our ex-wives, but also on our children, families and friends, that knew us both. I wish that I could tell you that you can both keep the same friends you had when you were married but they will be divided up like your assets. It's simply a fact. So many things will change in your life. I touched on a lot of them here but many of them can only be seen through your eyes.

An even higher percentage of second marriages end in divorce. Getting married a second time, honestly scares the hell out of me. I guess that you just have to have the faith of a child and the wisdom to learn from earlier mistakes to make it work.

At the end of each chapter, I intentionally always wrote, “Remember, you’re not alone in this even if sometimes you think you are.” I mean that.

Please share some of your experiences and suggestions on my website: divorced-men.com. Post any dating tips, recipes or experiences that you’d like to share. Note that I reserve the right to edit them and I don’t condone violence at all with regard to women. I hope that my site benefits other men (not in a gay way) so that we can make this transformation easier for those that are in it too. I'm not a doctor or counselor but I will try to answer any questions or give you any advice that I can.

For the last time, please remember, you're not alone in this even if sometimes you think you are.

Donna,

You'd better <u>never</u> fall for any of the 'guy' moves! LOL.

Love ya,

17502123R00105

Made in the USA
Charleston, SC
14 February 2013